SENSATIONAL SUCCULENTS

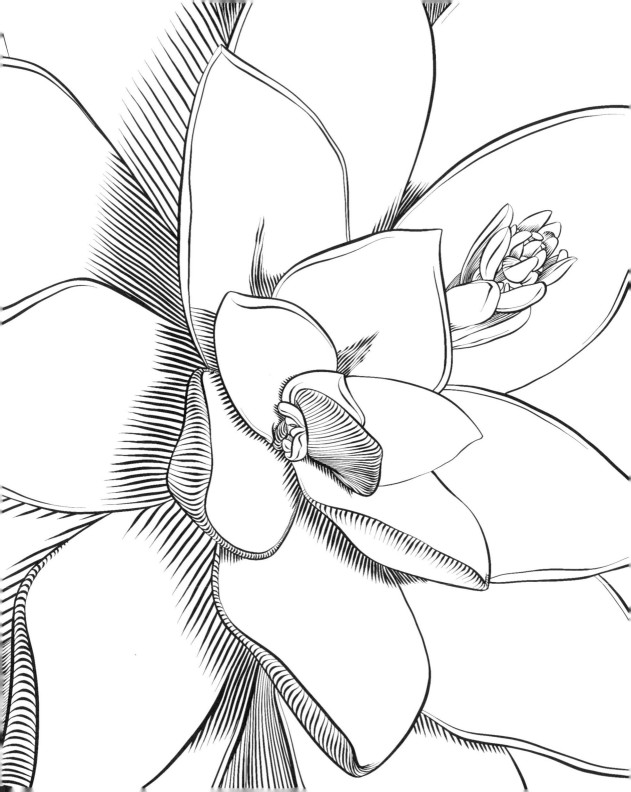

SENSATIONAL
SUCCULENTS

An adult coloring book of
amazing shapes and magical patterns

From the Queen of Succulents
DEBRA LEE BALDWIN
with illustrations by
LAURA SERRA

TIMBER PRESS ⫽ PORTLAND, OREGON

SUCCULENTS, like seashells and snowflakes, embody nature's exquisite patterns and geometry. To provide the images for this book, I sorted through hundreds of photos, selecting those that present succulents at their most beautiful. Berlin-based artist and illustrator Laura Serra transformed my images into the inspiring drawings on these pages. Now it's your turn! Take these gorgeous plants to the next level by creating artworks that perfectly express your taste and style. Happily, succulents come in all colors—including sky blue, lavender, teal, orange, and chartreuse—so feel free to use a variety of hues and to create dramatic combinations. As you bring these drawings to life, you'll participate in a transcendent process: making already lovely plants even more so. It's an honor to provide inspiration for your artistry! Do share your results and view those of others at https://www.pinterest.com/debraleebaldwin/ succulent-coloring-book-art/.

—DEBRA LEE BALDWIN

Aeoniums

Agave 'Blue Flame' and *Agave* 'Blue Glow'

Agave pelona

Aloes, coppertone stonecrop, and burro tail (*Sedum burrito*)

Kalanchoe tomentosa 'Chocolate Soldier', *Kalanchoe orgyalis*, and *Sedum* 'Dragon's Blood'

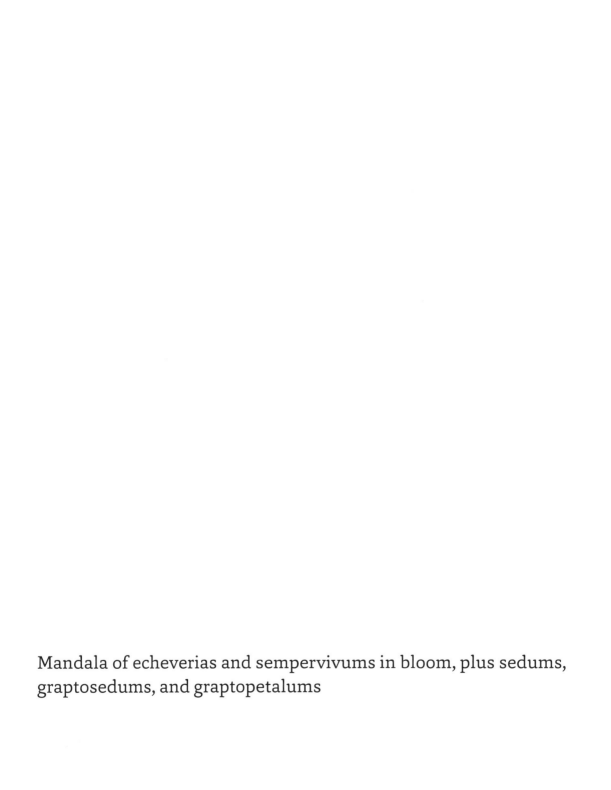

Mandala of echeverias and sempervivums in bloom, plus sedums, graptosedums, and graptopetalums

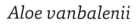

Aloe vanbalenii

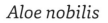

Aloe nobilis

Orostachys malacophylla var. *iwarenge*

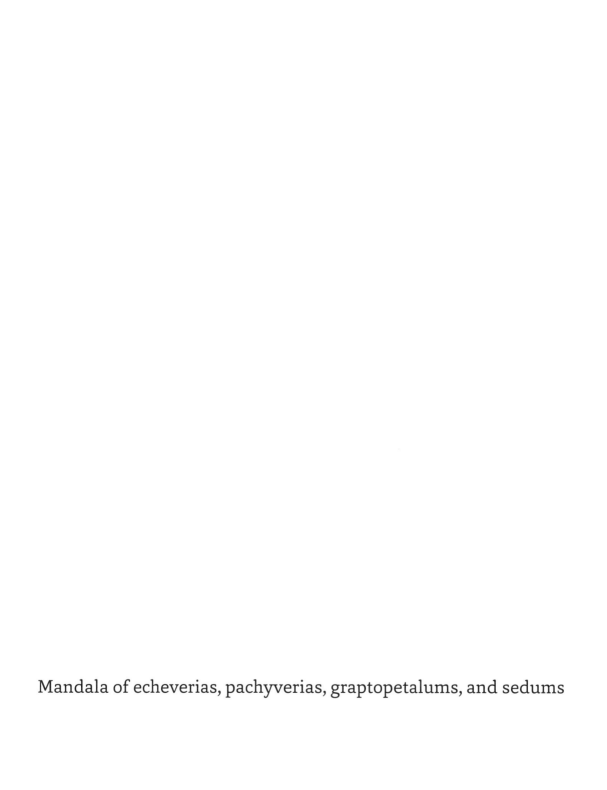

Mandala of echeverias, pachyverias, graptopetalums, and sedums

Euphorbia gorgonis

'Campfire' crassula, echeverias, aeoniums, sempervivums, haworthias, and sedums

Aeoniums and sempervivums with jade (*Crassula ovata*), *Sedum* 'Tricolor', and graptosedums

Pachyveria species

Mandala of echeverias and fenestraria

Euphorbia 'Snowflake'

Aeonium 'Kiwi'

Crassulas and aeoniums

Cremnosedum 'Little Gem'

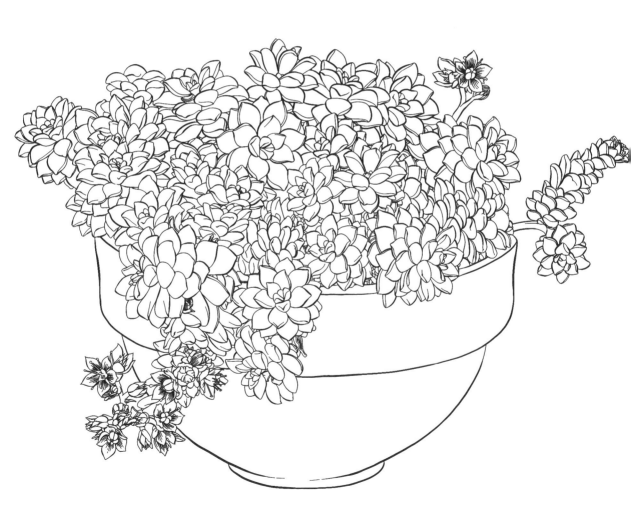

Ruffled echeveria cultivar

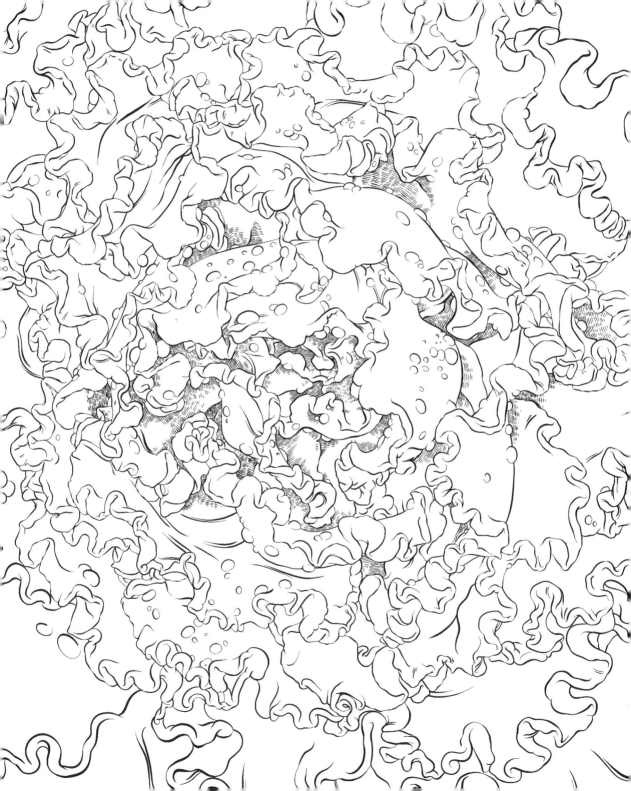

Graptoveria 'Opalina'

Aeoniums, graptoverias, sedums, echeverias, haworthias, crassulas, and kalanchoes

Echeveria hybrid

Agave attenuata (in pot), *Kalanchoe tubiflora*, ceroid (columnar) cacti, *Graptoveria* 'Fred Ives', and *Agave* 'Blue Glow'

Sedum rubrotinctum 'Pork and Beans'

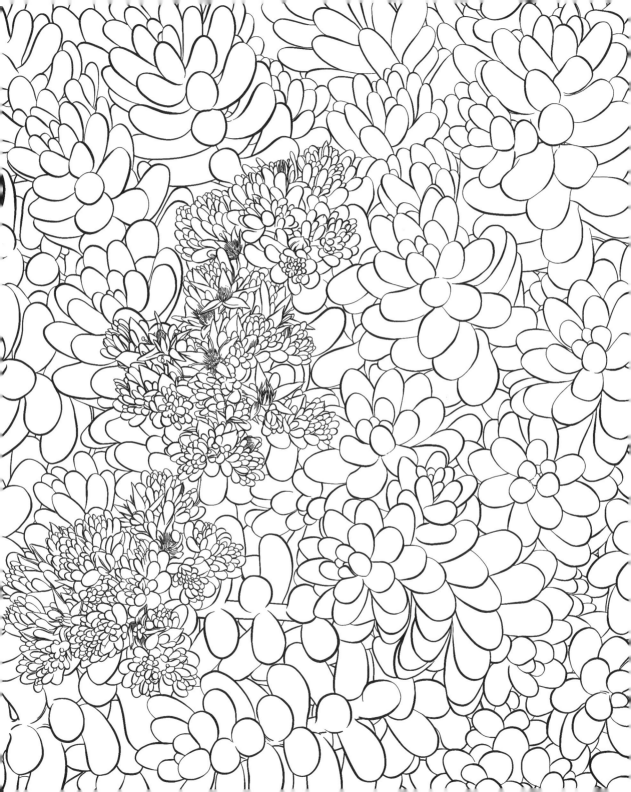

Echeverias, sedums, sempervivums, and pachyphytums

Ruffled echeveria cultivars

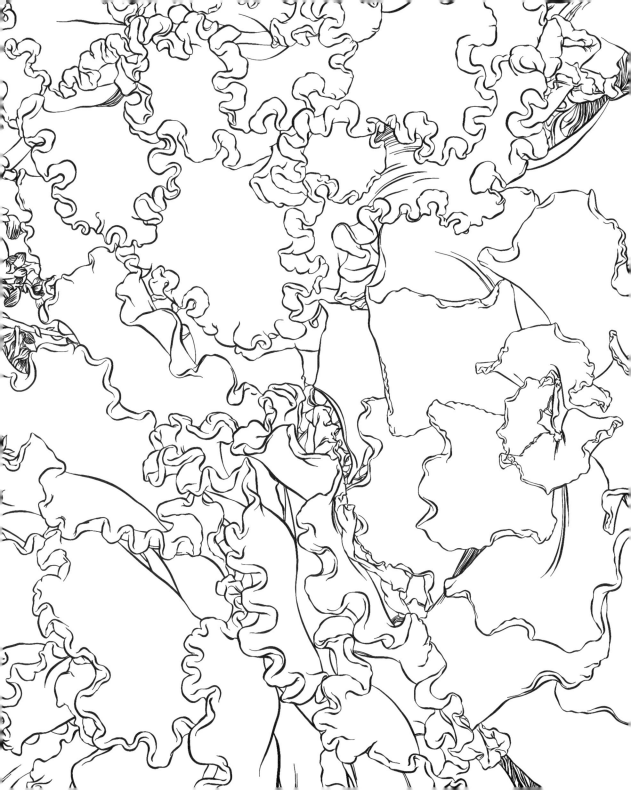

Graptoveria 'Fred Ives'

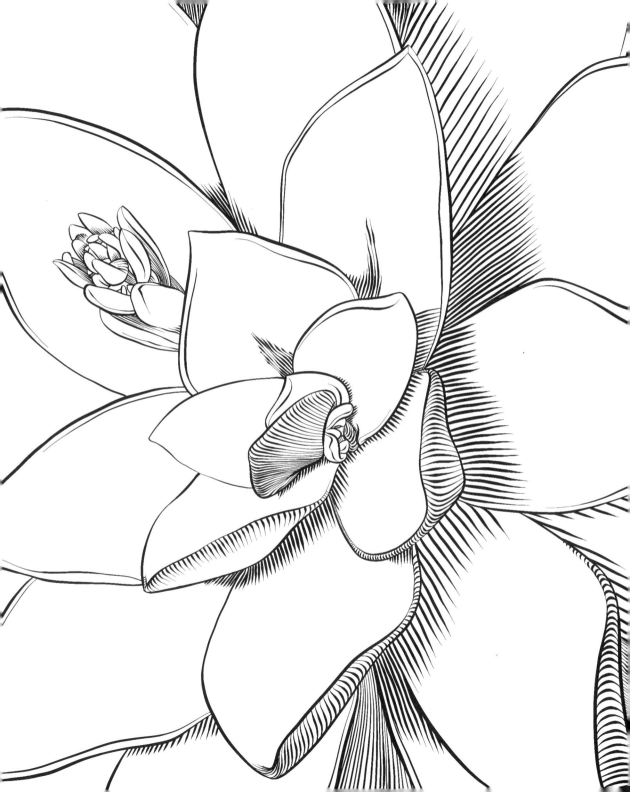

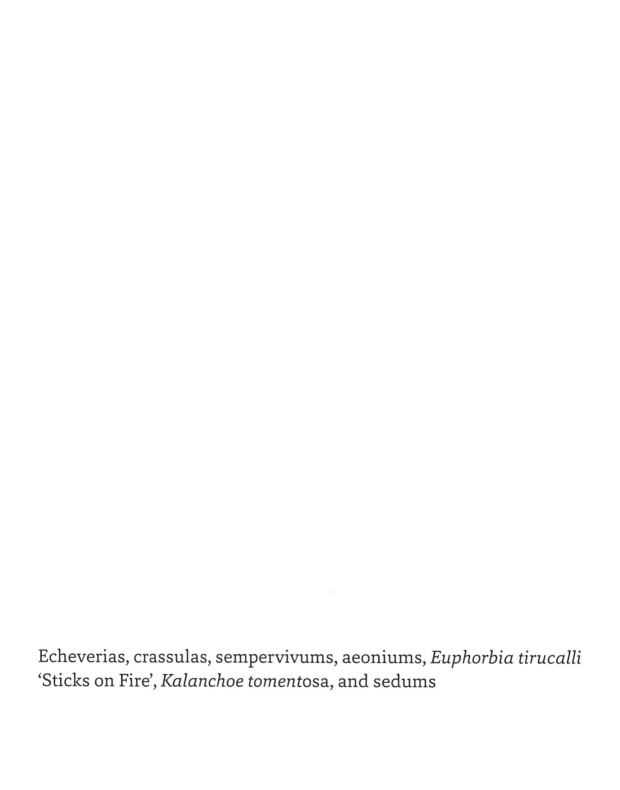

Echeverias, crassulas, sempervivums, aeoniums, *Euphorbia tirucalli* 'Sticks on Fire', *Kalanchoe tomentosa*, and sedums

Crested aeoniums

Agave parryi 'Truncata', *Mangave* 'Blood Spot', *Agave* 'Blue Glow', *Agave victoriae-reginae*, *Agave* 'Cream Spike', *Echeveria* 'Afterglow', and *Crassula* 'Campfire'

Sempervivums, *Cremnosedum* 'Little Gem', and *Crassula* 'Campfire'

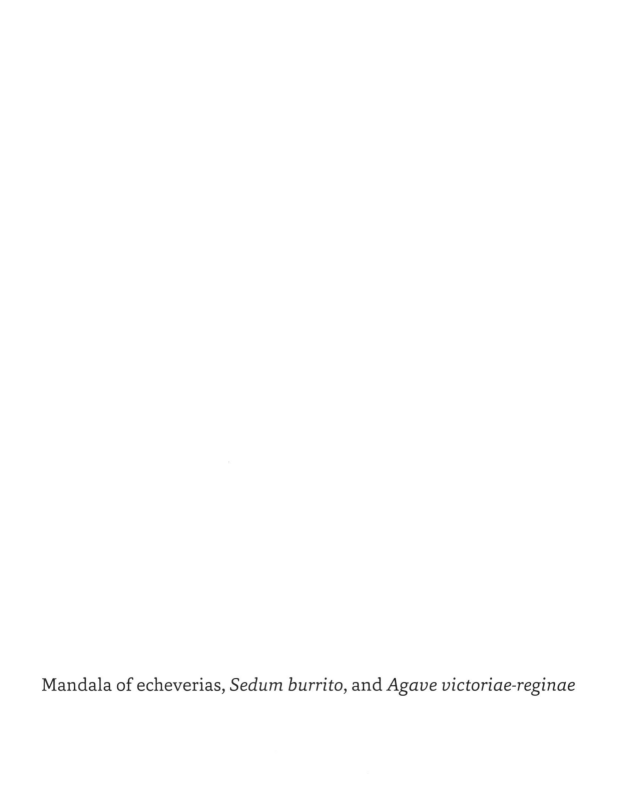

Mandala of echeverias, *Sedum burrito*, and *Agave victoriae-reginae*

Mandala of sedums and dwarf aloes

Aloe brevifolia

Echeveria hybrid

Agave parryi 'Truncata'

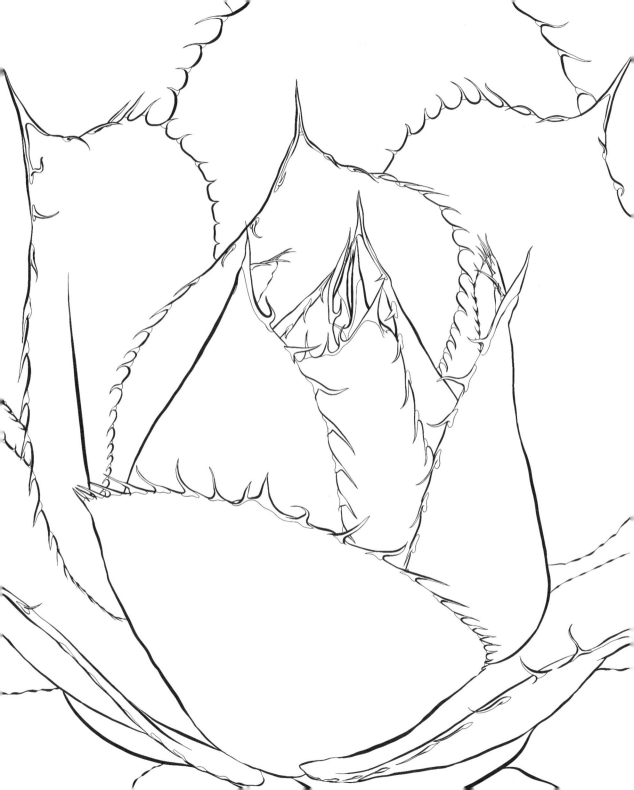

Sedum 'Angelina', *Sedum rubrotinctum* 'Pork and Beans', and *Crassula perforata*

Echeveria cultivars

Lithops species

Echeveria 'Neon Breakers'

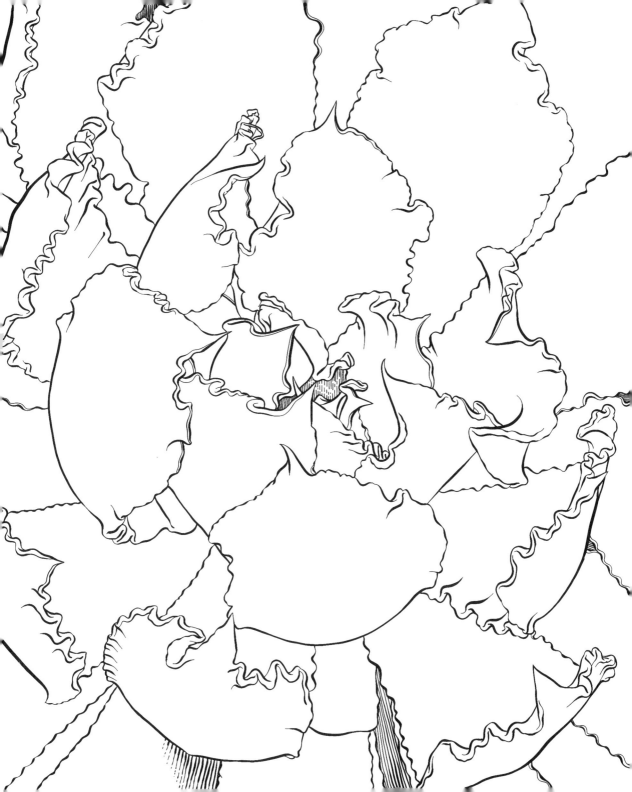

Kalanchoe luciae

Sempervivum species

Echeverias and sedums

Agave americana 'Marginata', *Crassula tetragona,*
Sansevieria trifasciata, and coppertone stonecrop

Agave 'Cream Spike'

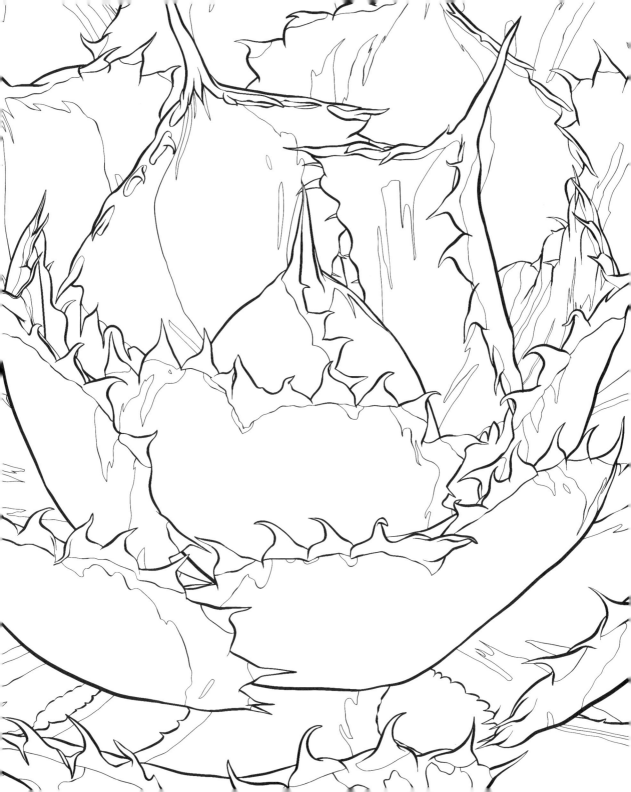

Echeverias and sempervivums

Cactus, dwarf aloes, crassula, and sempervivums

Echeveria 'Topsy Turvy'

Mandala of echeverias, sedums, and *Euphorbia tirucalli*
'Sticks on Fire'

Aloe vaombe

Mandala of *Agave lophantha* 'Quadricolor' and sedums

Agave potatorum and *Graptosedum* 'California Sunset'

Aloe capitata hybrid

Aloe dorotheae

Agave 'Blue Glow' and *Agave parryi* 'Truncata'

Mandala of crassulas and *Euphorbia tirucalli* 'Sticks on Fire'

Aeonium 'Sunburst'

Sedum burrito

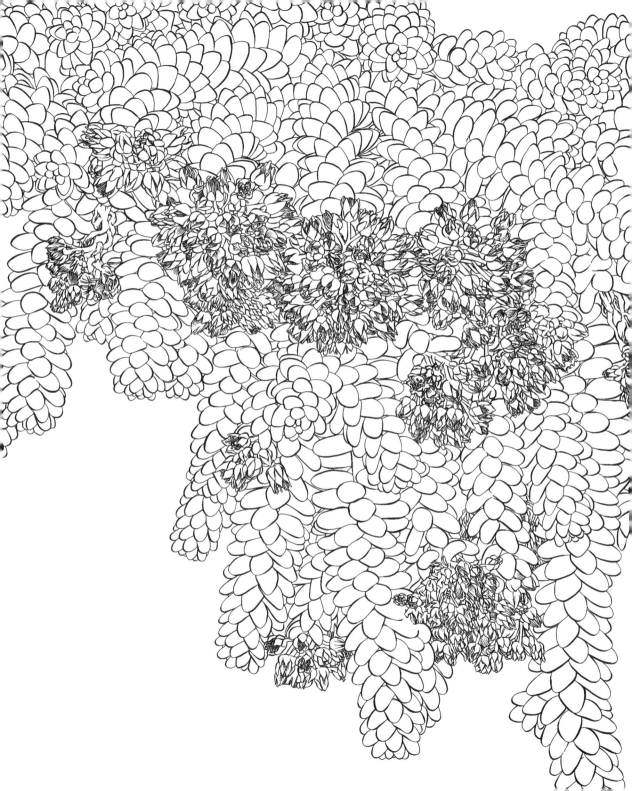

Euphorbia 'Snowflake'

Aloe humilis, Kalanchoe tomentosa 'Chocolate Soldier', and sedum

Sempervivum cultivar

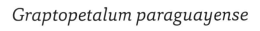

Graptopetalum paraguayense

Aeonium 'Party Platter'

Cactus pot

Graptopetalum paraguayense

Gasteraloe 'Green Ice', *Echeveria* hybrid, *Sedum dasyphyllum*, string of pearls (*Senecio rowleyanus*)

Agave victoriae-reginae

Ferocactus species

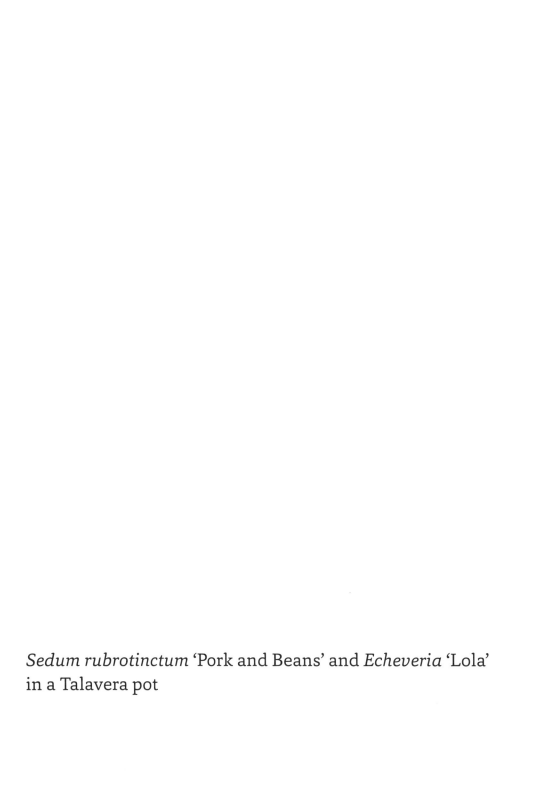

Sedum rubrotinctum 'Pork and Beans' and *Echeveria* 'Lola'
in a Talavera pot

Spiral aloe (*Aloe polyphylla*)

Variegated *Agave americana*

Agave lophantha 'Quadricolor'

Crassula capitella

Echeverias, aeoniums, graptopetalums, crassulas, and
cryptanthus bromeliads

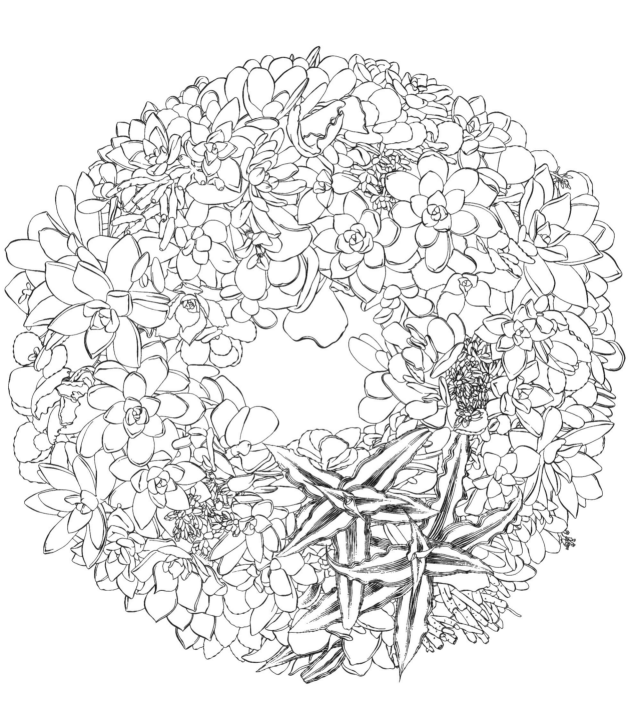

ED GOHLICH

LAURA SERRA

Debra Lee Baldwin—also known as the Queen of Succulents—wrote the Timber Press bestsellers *Designing with Succulents, Succulent Container Gardens,* and *Succulents Simplified.* Debra shares the exquisite aesthetics of succulents in everything she does, including her books, photos, videos, newsletters, presentations, and watercolor paintings. Learn more at debraleebaldwin.com.

The child of Sardinian immigrants, **Laura Serra** was raised in a small German town at the border of France. She began drawing at the age of two and never stopped. Her work has always been influenced by two seemingly unrelated subjects: typography and portraiture. With pencil, paint, ink, thread, pixels, markers, and coffee, Laura explores the relationships between characters and curves, letters and faces. See more of her work at lauraserra.org/.

Published in 2016 by Timber Press, Inc.

The Haseltine Building
133 S.W. Second Avenue, Suite 450
Portland, Oregon 97204-3527
timberpress.com

Printed in the United States

Book design and lettering by Patrick Barber

ISBN 13: 978-1-60469-746-9